ANIMAL WISE

Stripes, Spots, or Diamonds

A Book About Animal Patterns

by Patricia M. Stockland
illustrated by Todd Ouren

Special thanks to our advisers for their expertise:

Zoological Society of San Diego
San Diego Zoo
San Diego, California

Susan Kesselring, M.A., Literacy Educator
Rosemount-Apple Valley-Eagan (Minnesota) School District

PICTURE WINDOW BOOKS
Minneapolis, Minnesota

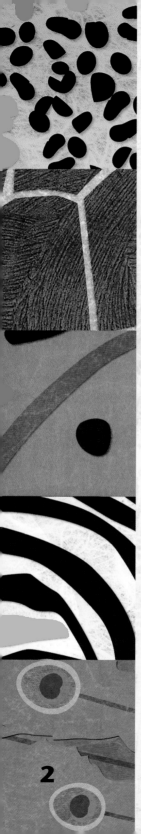

Managing Editor: Catherine Neitge
Creative Director: Terri Foley
Art Director: Keith Griffin
Editor: Christianne Jones
Designer: Todd Ouren
Page production: Picture Window Books
The illustrations in this book were prepared digitally.

Picture Window Books
5115 Excelsior Boulevard
Suite 232
Minneapolis, MN 55416
877-845-8392
www.picturewindowbooks.com

Printed in the United States of America.

Library of Congress Cataloging-in-Publication Data
Stockland, Patricia M.
Stripes, spots, or diamonds : a book about animal patterns /
by Patricia M. Stockland ; illustrated by Todd Ouren.
p. cm. — (Animal wise)
Includes bibliographical references (p.   ) and index.
ISBN 1-4048-0934-1 (hardcover)
1. Camouflage (Biology)—Juvenile literature. I. Ouren, Todd, ill.
II. Title.

QL759.S735 2004
591.47'2—dc22
2004020801

Pattern Adaptations

Adapting is a great way to survive. Patterns are one way that animals adapt to their environment. So how do patterns help animals live in the wild?

Some animals use their patterns to hide from their predators. Others use their patterns to sneak up on their prey. There are even animal patterns that scare other animals.

Find out why some animals have patterns and what they do with those wild spots or stripes.

Zebra

Black and white stripes zigzag and zoom across the plains. The stripes look blurry as the zebras run.

The black and white stripes help the zebra stand out so other animals stay away. When the zebra is with its herd, all of the stripes make it hard for a hungry lion to see the animals separately. They look like one big animal.

Each zebra has its own unique pattern of stripes. No two zebras are exactly alike.

Siberian Tiger

Sneaky, shadowy stripes hide in the tall grass. The Siberian tiger quietly waits.

This big cat uses its stripes to catch food. The stripes hide the tiger as it moves toward its meal. Animals can't see the tiger in the tall grass and trees. The tiger suddenly pounces from out of the shadows—*gotcha!*

All tigers have stripes. Depending on where they live, their stripes might be darker or lighter. Some tigers are white with black stripes.

Ladybug

Round, black spots cover a bright red back. Ladybug spots are easy to spy.

The ladybug uses these marks and colors as a warning sign to protect itself. Predators know the bold spots mean that ladybugs are not a tasty meal.

Not all ladybugs have spots. Some are just one solid color.

Leopard

Stunning spots sit high in a tree. The leopard looks down from its perch.

These spots help the leopard hide while it waits for prey. The sunlight shines through the leaves. It makes shadows that look like leopard spots. The leopard blends in with the shadows.

Black panthers are leopards, too. Their skin and fur have lots of dark pigment. This makes it very difficult to see a panther's spots.

Diamondback Rattlesnake

Dusty diamonds slither through the sandy desert. The diamondback rattlesnake shakes its tail.

This dry, scaly creature uses the diamonds on its back to blend in to rugged surroundings. This camouflage helps the diamondback hide from prey and escape predators.

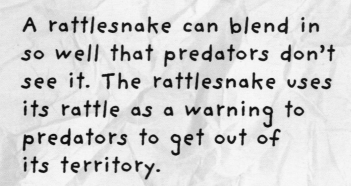

A rattlesnake can blend in so well that predators don't see it. The rattlesnake uses its rattle as a warning to predators to get out of its territory.

Pineapple Fish

Yellow wedges wiggle through the water. The pineapple fish swims on to the scene.

The fish's black-edged scales act like body armor. This pattern of tiny plates is tough—and sharp! Each scale ends with a pointy spine. Not many predators want to tackle the pineapple fish.

The lower jaw of the pineapple fish glows orange during the day and blue-green at night.

Peacock

Circles of green and blue scatter on colored feathers. The finely feathered peacock spreads his fan.

This bird uses these colorful feathers to attract a mate. When a female arrives, the peacock lifts his tail to lift the dazzling dots into a large fan. If the female is impressed, she'll choose him as a mate.

Female peacocks are called peahens. They don't have fancy patterns, colors, or fans. Being plain helps them hide when they nest.

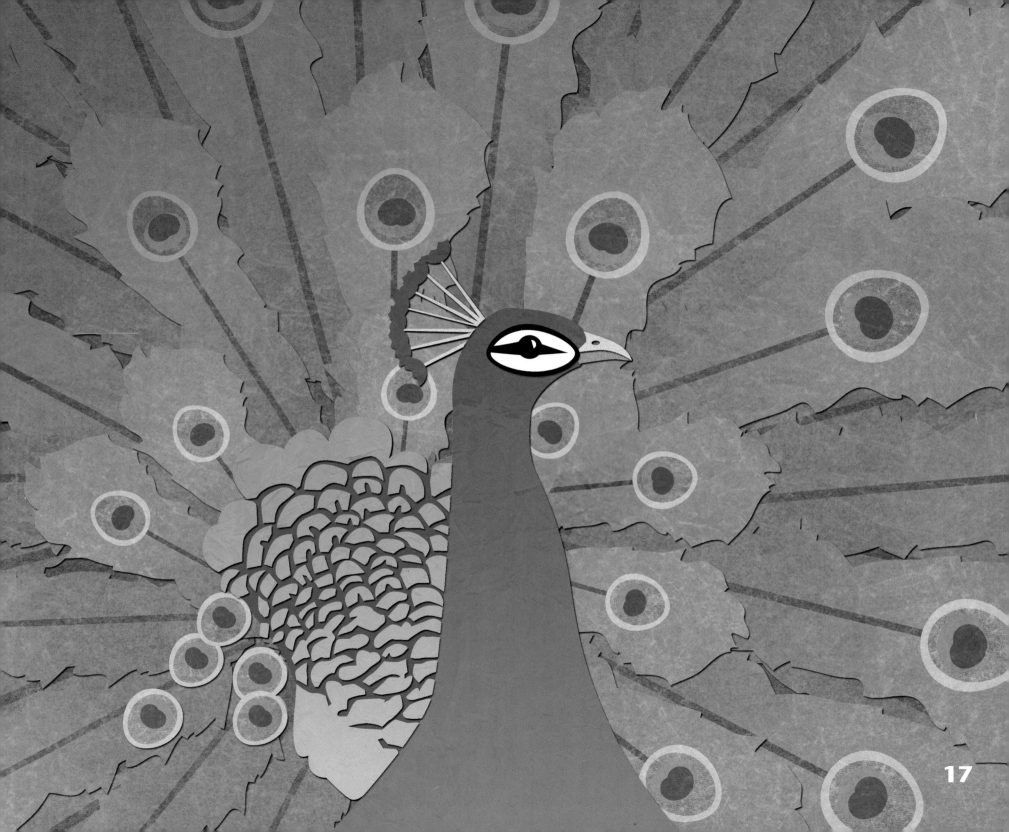

Blue-ringed Octopus

Bright, blue circles flash in the dark water. The blue-ringed octopus warns a predator.

You can't always see the blue rings on this tiny sea creature. The octopus only flashes its bright blue circles when it feels threatened or is about to attack. The rest of the time, the blue-ringed octopus hides its pattern.

The blue-ringed octopus is very small. The body of an average adult is about as big as a golf ball.

Painted Turtle

A pretty pattern of lines covers a tough shell.
The painted turtle rests by the pond.

Painted turtles carry protection on their backs.
Their shells have separate sections. Each section
is part of a pattern that makes the shell harder
to break. When a predator attacks, the tiny turtle
tucks itself inside.

The different shields
that make up a turtle's
shell are called scutes.
The shell usually has
54 scutes.

Do You Remember?

Point to the picture of the animal described in each question.

1. Females love the bright circles on my tail. These pretty feather patterns help me find a mate. Who am I?

   (peacock)

2. My diamonds aren't for jewelry. They help me blend in to the dry desert around me. Who am I?

   (diamondback rattlesnake)

3. My stripes are sneaky. I hide in tall grass, and my prey doesn't see me. Who am I?

   (Siberian tiger)

 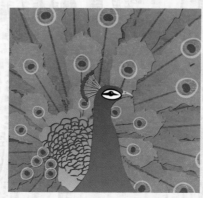 

22

Fun Facts

Siberian tigers are the biggest, strongest cats in the world.

Ladybugs eat aphids, which are little insects that harm plants. In this way, ladybugs are very helpful to farmers and gardeners.

To hide from predators, a painted turtle might bury itself in the mud.

Baby peacocks are called peachicks. All peacocks, male and female, are called peafowl.

The bite of a blue-ringed octopus can kill a person in 15 minutes.

Glossary

camouflage—a disguise that keeps an animal from being seen, or markings that make an animal look like something else

herd—a group of animals

organ —a body part that does a certain job, like a heart

pattern—shapes or colors that repeat in some order

pigment—a substance that gives an animal its color

predators— animals that hunt and eat other animals

prey—an animal that is hunted by another animal for food

territory—the special area in which an animal lives

TO LEARN MORE

At the Library

Kalman, Bobbie. *How Do Animals Adapt?* St. Catharines, Ontario: Crabtree Publishing, 2000.

Swinburne, Stephen R. *Lots and Lots of Zebra Stripes: Patterns in Nature.* Honesdale, Pa.: Boyds Mill Press, 1999.

Whitehouse, Patricia. *Zoo Patterns.* Chicago: Heinemann, 2002.

On the Web

FactHound offers a safe, fun way to find Web sites related to this book. All of the sites on FactHound have been researched by our staff. *www.facthound.com*

1. Visit the FactHound home page.
2. Enter a search word related to this book, or type in this special code: 1404809341
3. Click the FETCH IT button.

Your trusty FactHound will fetch the best Web sites for you!

INDEX

blue-ringed octopus, 18, 23
circles, 16, 18, 22
diamondback rattlesnake, 12, 22
diamonds, 12, 22
ladybug, 8, 23

leopard, 10
lines, 20
painted turtle, 20, 23
peacock, 16, 22, 23
pineapple fish, 14
predator, 3, 8, 12, 14, 18, 20, 23

prey, 3, 10, 12, 22
scales, 12, 14
Siberian tiger, 6, 22, 23
spots, 3, 8, 10
stripes, 3, 4, 6, 22
zebra, 4

Look for all of the books in the Animal Wise series:

Pointy, Long, or Round
A Book About Animal Shapes

Sand, Leaf, or Coral Reef
A Book About Animal Habitats

Stripes, Spots, or Diamonds
A Book About Animal Patterns

Red Eyes or Blue Feathers
A Book About Animal Colors

Strange Dances and Long Flights
A Book About Animal Behavior

Swing, Slither, or Swim
A Book About Animal Movements